JOURNEY TO THE LIGHT
A CELEBRATION OF ADVENT

by Don Besig & Nancy Price

Contents:

*Optional instrument obbligatos, congregational pages and narration are found on the Enhanced Listening CD-ND6021

Harold Flammer
MUSIC

A Division of Shawnee Press, Inc.
1107 17th Avenue South • Nashville, TN 37212

Visit Shawnee Press Online at www.shawneepress.com

FOREWORD

In the liturgical calendar, the Christian year begins with the season of Advent - a four week period of anticipation and preparation for the birth of Christ. **JOURNEY TO THE LIGHT** contains seven musical selections which have been widely and successfully used by churches of many denominations. These have been woven into a program with narration which may be performed as a part of regular worship or may be expanded by adding other elements such as prayers and congregational singing to create a special service. If performed early in the season, it will serve as a reminder of the special place that Advent holds in the traditions and teachings of the Christian church.

The music in the collection can also be performed as individual anthems. They are accessible to choirs of all sizes and can be easily prepared. **"Candles of Advent"** can be used throughout the season as part of the tradition of the Advent wreath. Each week, as a new candle is lit, the appropriate verse can be sung by the choir with the congregation joining on the refrain. **"Walk in the Light"** can also be sung as an Advent benediction response. Reproducible congregational parts, a copy of the narration and flute parts for several of the anthems are included on the Enhanced Listening CD.

It is our hope that you will adapt **JOURNEY TO THE LIGHT** to meet the specific needs of your church, and provide an opportunity for your congregation to focus on the wonderful feelings of expectation and anticipation that the Advent season provides.

Blessings . . .

Nancy Price and Don Besig

JOURNEY TO THE LIGHT
A Celebration of Advent

Reader 1:   There was a prophecy.
It had been passed from generation to generation by faithful believers. Through years of challenge and conflict, despair and dismay, the people of God watched and waited for a sign they knew would come.

Reader 2:   From the dark shadows that sometimes invaded their souls and threatened to shake their faith, a great light would break forth into all the world. Their lives would be filled with expectation and fulfillment, redemption and grace.

Reader 1:   There was a promise - God's promise - delivered through the words of the prophet Isaiah:

(Isaiah 9:6-7) **For to us a child is born, to us a son is given; and the government will be upon his shoulder, and his name will be called "Wonderful Counselor, Mighty God, Everlasting Father, Prince of Peace." Of the increase of his government and of peace there will be no end.**

Reader 2:   They watched and waited - preparing their hearts to welcome the Promised One who would restore hope, establish peace, share love and bring joy to all on earth.

THE PROMISE OF ADVENT

for S.A.T.B. voices, accompanied

Words by DON BESIG
and NANCY PRICE (ASCAP)

Music by
DON BESIG (ASCAP)

Through-out_ a trou-bled world, we wait_ to see a sign to give us hope and cour-age, to

and cast a - way all doubt and fear.

Ac -

cord - ing to the Word, our God__ will send a

son to bring us all sal - va - tion, to join us all as one._____ Ac - cord - ing to the Word, this child__ that heav - en

sends will live and reign for - ev - er,

and make us whole once a - gain.

*I - sa - iah once fore - told it, God's

* Tune: ES IST EIN' ROS', *Alte Catholische Geistliche Kirchengesäng, 1599;* alt.

prom - ise of a king.

Soon, we will all be - hold Him, and know_____ the peace He

brings. This child of hum - ble

birth___ will change the world for - ev - er,___

shar - ing God's love___ with

all on earth.___

Reader 1: Unlike those early people of faith who waited for the coming of the Messiah, we have seen and heard the wondrous story of the baby whose birth fulfilled the prophecy. We know that God's promise to send his son to live among the people on earth is true, and that we have been changed forever by his presence.

Reader 2: With the fast pace of our busy lives, it is often difficult to find time to capture the true feeling of Advent - a season of longing and hope, a time of anticipation and preparation for the coming of the promised Messiah. It is a spiritual journey that leads us out of darkness into the light of life. The prophet Isaiah wrote, "The people who walk in darkness will see a great light." We enter into this time secure in the knowledge that the Light is indeed among us.

Reader 1: Our journey begins with HOPE.

Even as faithful believers, we share some of the uncertainty and despair that surrounded God's people as they anxiously awaited the Savior's birth. We live in hope each day as we look forward to welcoming the long-expected king who will lead us in the one true way. Through the words of the prophets, God reaffirms the promise that Emmanuel will appear and dwell among us.

Reader 2: *(Isaiah 11:1-2)* **There shall come forth a shoot from the stump of Jesse, and a branch shall grow out of his roots. And the Spirit of the Lord shall rest upon him, the spirit of wisdom and understanding, the spirit of counsel and might, the spirit of knowledge and the fear of the Lord.**

The hope in our hearts is rekindled by the knowledge that God will send us the Light, provide for our every need and help us through whatever challenges we may face.

WAITING FOR THE LIGHT!

for S.A.T.B. voices, unaccompanied

Words by DON BESIG
and NANCY PRICE (ASCAP)

Music by
DON BESIG (ASCAP)

33

pare the way be-fore___ Him as the time is draw-ing near,___ for

37 SOLO

The

soon the true Mes-si - ah will ap-pear.___

ap - pear, He will ap-pear.___

41

earth will ring with glo - ry, and heav-en's light will shine.

Oo___ We will

45

know that God___ has sent us all a sign. So we are

sign.___

Reader 1: Our journey is blessed with PEACE.

Much like the people of Israel who knew many hardships and years of strife, the world we live in is filled with conflict. All around us are signs of anger, hatred, greed and distrust. Personal relationships, communities, and entire countries are damaged by people's inability to resolve differences through tolerance, understanding and compromise. Peace is something that we long to experience, but at times it seems to be an unattainable dream. Isaiah spoke of one who would come with righteousness and faithfulness.

Reader 2: *(Isaiah 40:1-2)* **Comfort, comfort my people, says your God. Speak tenderly to Jerusalem, and cry to her that her warfare is ended, that her iniquity is pardoned, that she has received from the Lord's hand double for all her sins.** *(Isaiah 11:6)* **The wolf shall dwell with the lamb, and the leopard shall lie down with the kid, and the calf and the lion and the fatling together, and a little child shall lead them.**

We wait patiently, for we have been promised a Prince of Peace who will come into our world that we may know the true meaning of God's peace in our lives.

O COME, EMMANUEL

for S.A.T.B. voices, accompanied,
with optional flute (or C-instrument) *

Words by DON BESIG
and NANCY PRICE (ASCAP)

Music by
DON BESIG (ASCAP)

* Part for flute or C-instrument included on the Enhanced Listening CD - ND6021.

TENOR

BASS

Long we have wait - ed for You to ap - pear,_____ bring - ing us hope and calm - ing our fear._____ De -

scend now from heav'n a - mong us to dwell.

O come, O come, Em - man -

- u - el.

* Tune: HYFRYDOL, Roland Hugh Prichard (1811-1877), Words by Charles Wesley (1707-1788), alt.

lead___ us; fill us with the peace___ You bring.

Soon we'll see___ a new day dawn - ing; send a

sign___ for all___ to see. End___ our

darkness, doubt ___ and long - ing; come and set ___ our spir - its free.

O come, O come, Em - man - - u - el.

Reader 1: Our journey is shared with LOVE.

Every day we encounter people whose lives seem cold and empty. They are lonely and unfulfilled and have a hard time relating to other people and to the world around them. We all need to experience love in our lives. The love of family and friends supports and nurtures us and brings a sense of well-being, belonging, and contentment. But, above all, we need the everlasting love of God to make us complete and to enable us to reach out to others. As we share God's love through our words and acts of kindness, we will receive the greatest blessing in our own lives. Isaiah told of a loving Messiah who would come into the world to care for us as his own.

Reader 2: *(Isaiah 40:11)* **He will feed his flock like a shepherd, he will gather the lambs in his arms, he will carry them in his bosom, and gently lead those that are with young.**

The coming of Emmanuel represents the greatest gift of love that God could give the world. Let us prepare the way for his presence among us by opening our hearts to his love.

A LITTLE CHILD WILL COME TO LEAD US

for S.A.T.B. voices, accompanied,
with optional flute (or C-instrument) *

Words by DON BESIG
and NANCY PRICE (ASCAP)

Music by
DON BESIG (ASCAP)

Moderately (♩ = ca. 80)

* Part for flute or C-instrument included on the Enhanced Listening CD-ND6021.

bove,   and a lit - tle child will come to lead us with his

love.

love,   with his love.

(+ flute)

* Tune: VENI EMMANUEL, 12th Century, alt.

GA5107

lit - tle child will come to lead__ us; the world a - waits that

night. A lit - tle child will come to lead__ us and

dark - ness will turn__ to light! The joy - ful al - le -

lu - ias will ring in heav'n a - bove; and a

lit - tle child will come to lead us with his love, with his

love.

Reader 1: Our journey is celebrated with JOY.

With hope, peace and love in our hearts, we experience the unending joy of God's presence in our lives. Early believers longed for God to dwell with them and bring joy into their troubled lives. Though they were mired in slavery and experienced great suffering, they listened to the words of the prophet telling them to prepare the way for the king who would lead them forth to a better life where they would once again know joy.

Reader 2: *(Isaiah 40: 4-5, 9)* **Every valley shall be lifted up, and every mountain and hill be made low; the uneven ground shall become level, and the rough places a plain. And the glory of the Lord shall be revealed, and all flesh shall see it together, for the mouth of the Lord has spoken. Get you up to a high mountain, O Zion, herald of good tidings, lift up your voice with strength, O Jerusalem, herald of good tidings, lift it up, fear not; say to the cities of Judah, "Behold your God!"**

Too often our lives lack joy as well. We let problems overwhelm us and negativity overtake us. Like those believers before us, we need to prepare for the arrival of the one who can change the way we live. We know that God's promise is embodied in our Savior, and that we can only experience true joy when he lives in us and becomes our light.

WHEN EMMANUEL HAS COME

for S.A.T.B. voices, accompanied,
with optional oboe (or C-instrument)*

Words by DON BESIG
and NANCY PRICE (ASCAP)

Music by
DON BESIG (ASCAP)

* Part for oboe or C-instrument included on the Enhanced Listening CD-ND6021.

All the world is waiting for a king. Soon we will behold what the prophets have foretold.

wait - ing for God's Son.

wait - ing for God's Son.

Soon He will ap - pear for the time is draw - ing

near. Soon we all will greet the Prom - ised

One. There will be joy, joy, joy when Em - man - u - el has come.

Heav - en will re - joice and praise His name.

There will be joy, joy, joy when Em-

man - u - el___ has come, and the world will

nev - er be the same.___

unis.

unis.

(+oboe)

mf

All the world is waiting for an answer.

Wait-ing for an

All the world is waiting for a

an - swer.

(This section is optional. If it is omitted, go directly to page 52.)

Reader 1: Our journey leads us to the Advent wreath - a visible reminder of the Light that awaits us as we approach the miracle of Christmas. This circle of intertwined branches is a symbol of God's endless love and eternal grace. Each candle represents a pathway out of the darkness toward the light, and gives us time to reflect upon the true meaning of advent. The hope, peace, love and joy that we anticipate along the way are fulfilled by the birth of a child whose life touches the heart of every believer, and whose light will be the light of the world.

(As each verse is sung, a candle may be lit.
Choir sings verses; congregation joins for refrain.)

CANDLES OF ADVENT

for S.A.T.B. voices, accompanied,
with optional congregational refrain *

Words by DON BESIG
and NANCY PRICE (ASCAP)

Music by
DON BESIG (ASCAP)

* Part for congregation included on the Enhanced Listening CD-ND6021.

50

GA5107

Help us find the Prom-ised One; guide us to the

child who will come.

to m.5, p.49

to m.5, p.49

(play after final verse)

Reader 2: There was a prophecy. There was a promise. Those who watched and waited found fulfillment when God sent a son to live among us. As we celebrate the days of Advent, let us prepare our hearts and minds to welcome the Promised One. He will restore our hope, help us to find peace, teach us how to love and fill our spirits with joy. United in faith and purpose, let us go forth and walk in the light!

WALK IN THE LIGHT

for S.A.T.B. voices, accompanied,
with optional congregational refrain*

Words by DON BESIG
and NANCY PRICE (ASCAP)

Music by
DON BESIG (ASCAP)

* Part for congregation included on the Enhanced Listening CD-ND6021.

brings,_____ let us wait and watch with o - pen hearts to wel - come our Lord____ and King.

Walk in the light, walk in the light,_____